Original title:
Tropical Surrender

Copyright © 2025 Creative Arts Management OÜ
All rights reserved.

Author: Helena Marchant
ISBN HARDBACK: 978-1-80581-604-1
ISBN PAPERBACK: 978-1-80581-131-2
ISBN EBOOK: 978-1-80581-604-1

The Promise of an Island Dawn

On the shore, a coconut fell,
Its husk cracked like an old-time shell.
Crabs in suits dance on the sand,
With dance moves that are quite unplanned.

Sunbeams sneak through palms so wide,
Sipping juice, a joy we can't hide.
Laughter bubbles, a joyful sound,
Where chaos and calm can be found.

Sweet Releases in Paradise

Pineapple hats and flip-flop shoes,
The iguanas gossip, sharing clues.
Cocktail umbrellas take to the breeze,
Wobbling gently on sandy knees.

Squirrels work hard to crack their prize,
Singing tunes of coconut pies.
With every sip, a giggle has grown,
In this land where troubles are overthrown.

Where Silence Meets the Waves

The ocean whispers, 'take a nap',
While seagulls play a silly clap.
Flip-flops flop while sunbathers snooze,
In dreams of whales and tropical blues.

The sun slips down like melting cheese,
Rippling sunsets make hearts seize.
Nearby, a rooster struts with flair,
In this peaceful place, without a care.

Capturing the Spirit of the Tropics

Mangoes swing from overhead vines,
As sun-kissed bodies dance with pines.
Bamboo drums thump with a joyful beat,
As laughter spills like a summer treat.

Fireflies twinkle, a sparkling plight,
Colorful flip-flops are quite the sight.
In a hammock, dreams take their flight,
In this world, everything feels just right.

A Dancer's Leap into the Breeze

In a swirl of colors bright,
She leaps to greet the sunlight.
Feet like feathers, laugh and sway,
Who knew dance could save the day?

With a shimmy and a shake,
Catch the breeze, make it quake.
Frogs join in with ribbit songs,
Jellyfish are swaying along.

Palm trees giggle in the shade,
As she twists, the grass gets laid.
Her flip-flops fly; word to the wise,
Watch your toes, oh how they rise!

In the chaos, a crab beats time,
With sidesteps that feel like a rhyme.
Laughter echoes, bright and clear,
Best dance moves? Down here, my dear!

Breathing in the Essence of Life

Beneath the sky, a piña colada,
Sipping slow, it feels like nada.
Banana peels make a fine slide,
Watch your step—hope you don't glide!

The breeze whispers, stories told,
Honeyed sunsets, fiery gold.
Coconuts chuckle, ripe and round,
You'll find fruits fall without a sound.

With each breath, the day's delight,
Unruly laughter takes to flight.
Someone's hat now in a tree,
Oh, secret treasure—come, you see?

Breathing deep the joyful air,
Finding beauty everywhere.
And in the chaos, we just thrive,
Where silly dreams feel fully alive!

Entwined in Nature's Caress

Vines tangle, a game of tag,
Laughter bursts, a playful brag.
Butterflies challenge, catch me if you can,
A ladybug shouts, "You're my fan!"

A mango falls and hits the ground,
The laughter rises; joy abounds.
Squirrels chuckle in their race,
While we sit back, slacken grace.

Tickled by petals, a soft embrace,
With every sneeze, we find our space.
The sun plays peek-a-boo up high,
Oh, sweet nature, how you sly!

Here, the chaos finds its peace,
In greenery, our worries cease.
Losing shoes while chasing dreams,
Life's a dance, or so it seems!

Sun-Washed Souls

Sun hats yawn in the sandy drift,
Behind sunglasses, selfies lift.
Lima beans plotting a cheeky prank,
Pineapples giggle, what a dank!

A beach ball rolls, taking flight,
Kids chase shadows in the light.
"Catch me if you can!" they cry,
And seagulls laugh—oh my, oh my!

Waves crash down with a splashy cheer,
Squawking jokes for all to hear.
Flip-flops scattered like confetti,
Life's a party, don't be petty!

Each sandcastle a royal throne,
In this sun-washed world, we own.
With every wave, we find our role,
Sunshine tickles every soul!

Echoes of the Gentle Shore

Seagulls squawk, they steal my fries,
A crab walks by, with beady eyes.
Flip-flops flop, I dance with flair,
Sunburned nose, but who would care?

Waves crash down with a laugh so loud,
A beach ball bounces, joins the crowd.
Sandy hair, a sight to see,
Dancing with a palm tree's glee!

Unraveling the Mysteries of the Tropics

Beneath the palm, a secret's told,
How coconuts dance, the gossip's bold.
Monkeys tease from tangled vines,
While I sip juice, feel the sunshine.

A lizard slips, adds to the chill,
Did that wave just try to kill?
Mysteries live in every twist,
Like where on earth my keys are missed!

A Caress of Colorful Blooms

Petals pink, like a candy land,
Bees buzz around, oh isn't that grand?
A flower's giggle, sweet and low,
In this garden, laughter flows.

Yellow daisies winking bright,
Think they own this happy sight.
But here I stand, with a big grin,
In this bloom, I'll surely win!

The Melody of Distant Drums

Drums pound softly, a rhythmic tease,
I dance like fish in the swaying breeze.
Beat drops low, and so do I,
Tripping over waves, oh my, oh my!

A parrot squawks, it wants to play,
I think I'll join, it's a funny day.
Dance on sand, twirling with zest,
In this rhythm, I feel my best!

Undercurrents of Bliss

With a drink in my hand, I lost my flip-flop,
The waves take it far, I watch it plop.
Seagulls squawk loud, give me some sass,
I shout back at them, with a piece of grass.

Body surfing fails, I land on my back,
Salt in my eyes, what's my life's track?
The sun's blazing hot, yet I smile with glee,
Chasing crabs around, they look back at me.

Dreams in Paradise

I dreamt of coconuts falling from trees,
Instead a mango hit me, oh please!
In my hammock suspended, I drift off to play,
Waking up startled, it's the end of the day.

A pineapple piña colada turns real,
But I sip it too fast, and whoa, what a deal!
The umbrella's awry, my straw's in a twist,
At this point, I'm trapped; in fun, I persist.

Laughter Under the Palms

Palm leaves dance wildly, in the light breeze,
Twirling my hat off, oh how they tease!
Children run past with a sandcastle throne,
I wave at the crabs, who are now my own.

A parrot lands near, squawking "what's up?"
He steals my chips; I shout, "That's not good luck!"
Yet I toss him some fries, we're buddies now,
Feathers and laughter, joy takes a bow.

Isolated Sunsets

The sun dips low, dripping orange and pink,
My friend drops his ice cream, starts to rethink.
We laugh as it melts, a slippery sight,
Chasing down seagulls, it takes flight!

I trip on a sandbar, it's all quite absurd,
My dignity's lacking; it's too late to deter.
Yet waves keep on crashing, a giggle prevails,
In this goofy spell, joy beams like trails.

Island Whispers

On sandy shores where crabs do dance,
A mermaid laughs, not a second chance.
Her tail is stuck in an old flip-flop,
She wiggles hard, but the tide won't stop.

Parrots squawk in a gossip spree,
As we sip coconuts, feeling so free.
A sunburnt tourist wears socks with flair,
His flip-flops missing, lost to the air.

Sun-kissed Revelations

The sun is bright, like a toddler's grin,
As I chase a seagull, it jumps from the bin.
Beach balls collide with forgotten kids,
While I aim for gold but end up with twids.

Bikinis tangled, what a sight to behold,
As laughter erupts, turning red from the cold.
A sandcastle crowns a bewildered crab,
He wears it proud like a royal fab.

Lush Embrace of Dusk

The sunset glows with colors so wild,
As I trip on a flip-flop, and act like a child.
The hammock swings, a lullaby sweet,
But my snack attacks, and I can't take a seat.

Fireflies giggle, lighting the dark,
While I think I'm smooth, but miss the mark.
A drink spilled here, and a laughter there,
In this raucous dance, we float in the air.

Beneath the Palms of Desire

The coconuts fall, a game of chance,
One hits a coconut, ignites a new dance.
A sunhat flies, swirling in the breeze,
As I fumble my drink; oh, what a tease!

The breeze whispers softly, cheers to our plight,
While I dodge a crab that scuttles with might.
We laugh 'til we cry, what a silly show,
Underneath palm trees, we let all else go.

Reveling in the Warmth of the Day

Sunshine tickles my nose,
While I dance on my toes,
Lemonade in hand, feeling bold,
Napping in a hammock, tales told.

Flip-flops flapping by the sea,
Sandy toes and birds in glee,
An ice cream cone, oh what a sight,
Melts down my hand, a tasty plight.

Palm trees wave, they're my crew,
Coconuts fall, what a view!
Crabs join the jig, quite the show,
Under the sun, I steal the glow.

The Color of Longing

A sunset dip in hues so bright,
Fuzzballs dancing, what a sight,
Bikinis laughing on each curve,
In the warmth, we lose our nerve.

Pineapple socks, who would dare?
Sipping joy without a care,
A hammock swings with hints of fate,
As flirtatious breezes elevate.

Hands waving at clouds like friends,
With each breeze, the fun never ends,
Feeling waves tickle my hip,
Oh, the sweetness of this trip!

Whirlwind of Blossoms

Dancing petals swirl around,
Buzzing bees, a silly sound,
A flower crown atop my head,
Mixing colors where we tread.

Rose with lavender, oh my,
In a field where dreams can fly,
Sneezing pollen, oh what fun,
Allergies can't stop this run!

Laughing as I trip and whirl,
In a garden full of pearl,
Each bloom whispers secrets sweet,
While bees bring us their patron's greet.

Finding Nirvana in the Moment

Seagulls squawking, what a ruckus,
Joyful chaos, just like us,
Chasing shadows on the sand,
With a mind-less, carefree hand.

Finding bliss in a piña colada,
Undulating waves dance the cha-cha,
Melting popsicles on my lips,
Flavors bursting with silly quips.

Meditation? Nah, just a sigh,
As doughnuts fly up to the sky,
With every giggle, oh what a thrill,
In this moment, time stands still.

The Call of Paradise

In a hammock, dreams do sway,
With a coconut drink all day.
Monkeys steal my sunblock stash,
While I ponder getting a tan so brash.

Flip-flops flip, I trip and fall,
Spraying sand like a beach ball.
Seagulls laugh, oh what a sight,
Chasing crabs, it feels so right.

Lost in Verdant Embrace

The jungle whispers, "Take a peek!"
But my knee-deep in mud, oh what a weak!
Lizards dance on a leafy throne,
As I trip on roots, and it feels like home.

Ferns tickle my nose, oh what joy!
Silly me, a lost little boy.
A toucan squawks, wearing a grin,
In this green maze, let the fun begin!

Secrets Spun from Sea Foam

Waves crash down with a giddy cheer,
As I build castles that disappear.
A crab waves back with a tiny claw,
Oh, I'm the ruler, or so I saw.

In sea foam, I find treasures rare,
A shell that squeaks, beware the pair!
Fish giggle as they dart away,
Who knew the ocean could play this way?

Over the Moon and Under the Stars

Under the sky, a glow so bright,
I trip on jelly while dancing at night.
Fireflies blink in the dark with glee,
As I pretend to be part of the sea.

A serenade from frogs, so loud!
Trying to find my way through the crowd.
Over the moon, I spin and twirl,
In this wild night, I set the world!

The Lure of Wild Orchids

In a jungle of colors, I frolic with glee,
Sipping coconut juice as I dance with a bee.
Orchids whisper secrets in a sunbeam glow,
While my hat flies away, what a wonderful show!

With laughter and giggles, I stumble and trip,
Chasing bright butterflies but losing my grip.
The monkeys are chuckling, while hanging from trees,
As I barter with ants for my sandwich of cheese.

Sunlit Memories of Exploration

On a raft made of palm leaves, I drift and I sway,
With sunburned shoulders, I'm ready to play.
The fish all wink at me, "We're soft in the sea!"
While I splash like a seal, not quite as carefree.

A pelican swoops down, stealing my hat,
I shout, "Hey! Come back, you ungrateful brat!"
As it steals my sunblock and snacks for its crew,
I ponder on life - oh, what would my mother do?

Melting into Warmth

The sun hugs my skin, as I lie on the sand,
A popsicle drips, my fingers all planned.
With each licky bite, I'm lost in a trance,
But the seagull's cawing, interrupting my dance.

I roll in the warmth, like a pancake so fried,
Tacos in dreams, and guacamole inside.
With laughter I find, that I can't quite resist,
As I ride the big waves on a giant float fist.

Claws in the Sand

Crabs at the shoreline are scratching their backs,
While I build a castle with moats and some snacks.
They march like a troop, with a pinch and a tease,
I laugh at their antics, oh, what a breeze!

Their claws wave to me as if saying, "Join in!"
But I'm stuck in my bucket, where do I begin?
With a sandcastle army, our kingdom so grand,
With crabs as my knights, it's a perfect land!

The Language of the Coconut Palm

The palm waves hello, a breezy chat,
As coconuts giggle, like playful cats.
They whisper sweet secrets, in coconut tones,
With every soft rustle, they laugh at our phones.

A coconut fell with a tap and a thud,
'Guess I'm a fruit, not just lumber and mud!'
The locals all chuckle, 'It's a nutty affair,'
While sipping bright drinks with umbrellas to share.

Beneath their tall shade, we lounge and we grin,
As coconuts watch us, we feel like we win.
Their laughter cascades on the waves of the sea,
In the language of palms, we're all meant to be.

Resplendent Repose

Under the sun, where the hammocks sway,
I tried to nap, but my mind went astray.
A parrot squawked loudly, 'Wake up! Have some fun!'
While I dreamed of coconuts soaking in rum.

A lizard danced past with a cartoonish glee,
'Take a break!' it yelled, 'Join the party with me!'
With shades of bright green and a flair full of zest,
I gave in to laughter, and forgot all the rest.

The sand tickled toes while I lounged with a frown,
'Why is it too soft? I might sink to the ground!'
But with every good giggle that escaped from my cheek,
Life's resplendent repose is both silly and sleek.

Exploration of Hidden Waterfalls

With a splash and a laugh, we set off today,
In search of the falls where the rubber ducks play.
Around every corner, we giggled and slipped,
As bamboo grove monsters quietly dripped.

I tripped on a root, fell right on my bum,
And shouted, 'Don't worry! This is all part of fun!'
The waterfall beckoned, its voice was a tease,
Like a prankster it pooled, with a wink and a breeze.

We reached the grand falls, what a glorious sight!
Water danced down, spitting sparkles of light.
We splashed like young dolphins, with grins ear to ear,
Exploring these wonders, our laughter sincere.

Glistening Moments of Serenity

In a hammock strung low, I swayed to and fro,
With a drink in my hand, taking life nice and slow.
The sun kissed my toes while I blinked at the sky,
As clouds shaped like turtles drifted lazily by.

The breeze brought whispers of sweet coconut dreams,
While I plotted my next snack—maybe guava with creams.
A crab scuttled near, in a hat made of leaves,
It danced on the sand, oh, what trickery weaves!

With laughter as currency, these moments delight,
Like sparkle-flecked waves in the warm golden light.
Serenity glistens in antics we share,
In this quirky adventure, we float without care.

Heartbeats in the Jungle

In the jungle, I lost my shoe,
Monkeys laughed, what could I do?
A parrot squawked with all its might,
'This dance is fun, you're quite a sight!'

Vines tangled like a naughty friend,
My limbs are flailing, where's the end?
The toucans chuckled, oh so loud,
I'm the star of this silly crowd!

With every swing, I fear I'll fall,
The trees just giggle, oh what a brawl!
But laughter bubbles, and spirits soar,
In this green circus, we crave for more!

So join the show, leave worries behind,
Embrace the rhythm, be unconfined.
Swing like the vines, and dance with glee,
In this wild place, we're truly free!

A Symphony of Fragrance

A whiff of mango fills the air,
But watch out, it's a fruit affair!
The juice drips down, what a scene,
Sticky and sweet, like a sugar dream!

Flowers bloom in a vibrant spree,
Bees get buzzed, what's their decree?
The coconut laughs as it rolls away,
Chasing aromas, what a fun play!

The pineapples gossip, oh so bold,
Their spiky crowns wrapped in gold.
Bananas slip with a comic grace,
Peels flying high in this fruity race!

So let's dance in this aroma tale,
With giggles and scents, let's set sail.
In this garden, we find delight,
Where fragrance winks and brings pure light!

Secrets of the Coral Reef

Under the waves, fish make a fuss,
A clownfish rolls, says, "Catch the bus!"
With colors bright, they swirl and flip,
In this coral maze, let's take a trip!

Sea turtles glide with exaggerated flair,
"I'm late for brunch!" they declare with care.
Octopuses hide and play peek-a-boo,
Laughing at all of the things they do!

A crab with swagger, thinks he's a king,
Dancing on rocks, he starts to sing.
But watch your step, or you might be caught,
In a game of tag—oh, what a thought!

So join the fun in this watery place,
With giggles and splashes, keep up the pace.
Secrets abound in this ocean spree,
Where laughter echoes, and you're truly free!

When the Rain Kisses the Earth

Raindrops bounce like tinny drums,
The ground sighs deep, a tune that hums.
Puddles form like little lakes,
Splashing around, oh what mistakes!

Umbrellas dance, swaying to the beat,
With every gust, they skip on their feet.
Worms wriggle up, all slick and sly,
"What's the rush?" they seem to cry!

The thunder rumbles, a joke in the sky,
"Hold your horses, let's give it a try!"
A dog darts past, coat soaked and wild,
Finding a rainbow, it's nature's child!

So frolic and play in this joyful rain,
Where laughter mixes with all the gain.
When droplets fall, hearts overflow,
In this wet wonderland, let's steal the show!

Oasis of the Heart

In a land where pineapples grow,
And the iguanas steal the show,
I lounged on a float with my drink in tow,
Waves tickled my toes, oh what a glow!

The sun wore its hat, a big, silly grin,
As parrots in shades chirped, 'Let the fun begin!'
I tried to do yoga, fell right in the fin,
Of a friendly dolphin who said, 'Join in!'

Coconuts danced in a funny parade,
While crabs in tuxedos seemed less afraid,
I tiptoed around, trying not to invade,
Their jolly fiesta, under shade, well-played!

As night fell, the stars came out to play,
The moon cracked jokes, lit up the bay,
I told my troubles to the ocean, they'd sway,
And laughed till the dawn, in a carefree way!

Surrendering to the Tide

The ocean called out with a squeaky toy,
It said, 'Join the current, oh little buoy!'
With flip-flops in hand and my heart full of joy,
I leaped into waves like a giddy boy!

The fish wore bow ties, how chic and refined,
While jellyfish giggled, all tangled and twined,
I tried to catch one but the sea had me blind,
'More fun than a picnic!' was my heart's sign.

Seagulls dropped snacks that they swiped from a stand,
I fished for my lunch with a plastic spoon band,
As crabs critiqued my funny beach dance so grand,
I surrendered to laughter, they clapped all around!

With sunset's paintbrush, the sky danced with flair,
I rode on a wave, arms wide in the air,
Ocean's sweet whispers, cool breeze in my hair,
A surrender to joy, with naught left to bare!

Nature's Enchanted Lullaby

In a hammock hung low, I drifted away,
Where the palm trees murmured, 'Come, play and stay,'
With coconuts cracking their comedy play,
And crickets serenading at the end of the day.

My thoughts painted rainbows that twisted and spun,
While the sun's cheeky beams totally had fun,
A toucan named Tim, he joined on the run,
Declaring, 'Let's laugh 'til the night is all done!'

Frogs croaked in rhythm, a croaky delight,
As fireflies giggled, glowing up the night,
I danced with the shadows, absurdly polite,
Embracing the magic, conversational light.

With nature as sponsor, the laughter would flow,
While waves pirouetted in an elegant show,
The night kissed my worries, whisked them below,
In this enchanted realm, my spirit could grow!

Waves of Euphoria

Riding the crest of a bubbly delight,
With goggles and floaties, I took off in flight,
The waves giggled softly, a ticklish sight,
As I crashed in the foam, oh what a night!

A crab in a bowtie set up the game,
As conch shells debated who'd win the fame,
I dove in headfirst, 'This beach is insane!'
With every splash, I'd burst out my name!

The sun beamed brightly, a spotlight above,
While flamingo dancers boogied with love,
Drinks spilled around, oh, foolishly shoved,
All laughter exploded, a joyful glove.

So here comes the tide, in a swirl and a spin,
With laughter and madness, I welcomed it in,
As the sea brought its friends, like it knew all my kin,
In waves of pure joy, I'd gladly give in!

Serenity in the Breeze

Parrots squawk, the sun is high,
A beach ball flies, oh my, oh my!
Sandy toes and laughter loud,
I'll wear my hat, I'll feel so proud.

A coconut lands atop my head,
Why did I think this was my bed?
Frisbees dance, the piña colada's near,
I chase my drink, I scream with cheer!

With every wave, a splash of fun,
I'm sunburned and feeling like a bun.
The sun sets low, the sky aglow,
Last laugh of the day, let's steal the show!

In this paradise, my heart is free,
Underneath the swaying palm tree.
A life of whimsy is my decree,
Bring on the joy, come join with me!

Waves of Solace

The ocean giggles, it gives a flirt,
I delve in waves, then I do a spurt.
Flippers on, I swim like a fish,
Caught in seaweed, it's my new ambition!

Surfers ride like they own the day,
I wipe out and dance, it's my own ballet.
Seashell treasures fill my pouch,
Found a shoe — oh what a slouch!

Sunburned noses and honking seals,
My friends and I make foolish deals.
One lost flip-flop for a scoop of ice,
In waves of solace, life is nice!

As sunset paints the sky with flair,
We're jellyfish dodging, without a care.
In laughter's echoes, we'll always stay,
With salty kisses at the end of the day!

Chasing the Golden Horizon

Running fast, I trip on sand,
The golden ray rips from my hand.
It's just a trick, my eyes deceive,
But oh, the joy, I still believe!

Shells are treasures, they whisper tales,
Of mermaids lost, and windy gales.
I prance around like a goofy seal,
Sandy adventures are just my deal!

A seagull swoops, it wants my fries,
I toss it crumbs while I improvise.
With shades of gold, we chase the night,
Who knew surrender could be this light?

The horizon calls, it's aglow with fun,
I'll follow laughter, until I'm done.
With grains of joy tucked in my pocket,
I'll sail away from mundane's socket!

Secrets of the Mango Grove

In a grove of dreams, where mangos grow,
I try to balance, then take a low blow.
Sticky fingers, sweet and bright,
Caught in a fight with a pesky kite!

The breeze teases with whispers of cheer,
I laugh aloud, it's my favorite year.
Bumbles and tumbles, oh what a scene,
The mangoes judge, they're far too keen!

Underneath the shade, we sing off-key,
The mango pit toss, Oh, what a spree!
A squirrel joins in this merriment spree,
We'll toast to a life of absurdity!

Secrets told in the rustling leaves,
Forgotten lullabies put us at ease.
With half-smiles and wild mango stains,
We find our joy in silly refrains!

Under the Gaze of Palm Fronds

Swaying palms in summer's dance,
Laughing at my sunburned pants.
Coconuts fall with a plop,
As I dodge and do the hop.

Colorful drinks in hand, oh dear,
My hat flew off, disappeared!
I chase it down with a silly grin,
While tourists watch and dive right in.

Sunbathers wink from sandy beds,
Each toss of sand is full of threads.
A crab patrols my beach towel zone,
Claiming it now as his own throne.

Let's dance like waves, leap and spin,
Forget the rules, let the fun begin.
Under this sky, so wide and blue,
What else can we do but laugh and snooze?

Love Letters in the Breeze

The breeze carries whispers sweet,
As I trip over my own two feet.
Messages tucked inside palm leaves,
Mighty fine, but I can't believe!

With seashells scattered like thoughts,
I pen my feels, but tie up knots.
A lobster reads them with a sigh,
While I dub him my love spy.

The waves giggle, tickle my toes,
As I write more than my pen knows.
But the tide comes in, and away they float,
My feelings lost as I swat a gloat.

Yet still I laugh, what a fine jest,
To love a place and not the rest.
For every breeze has tales to share,
Of goofy love and sun-drenched air.

Whispers of the Island Breeze

Oh, the island sings a silly tune,
With crabs that boogie 'neath the moon.
Sea turtles laugh in the gentle surf,
A beachside dance with lots of mirth.

Waves brush my toes, they just can't wait,
For me to join this wacky fate.
Flying fish make a splashy leap,
While I stand still, in awe, and creep.

Gossip floats on each windblown gust,
As I toss my chips, who can I trust?
A seagull steals my last little fry,
And I just shake my head and sigh.

But here I am, dreaming wide awake,
In this sea of giggles, I'll never break.
Surrendered in this playful space,
With laughter and love, my kind of place.

Sun-Kissed Horizons

Horizons stretch with colors bright,
As I slip into the world of light.
Surfboards fly past, zipping fast,
While I munch on snacks, such a blast!

The sun smiles down with a wink,
As I sip my drink and start to think.
"Did my flip-flop just go rogue?"
A gecko nods, while I sit in a fog.

Friends pile in with laughter loud,
Making memories we're so proud.
But watch your drink, the ice might bolt,
And give your giggles quite a jolt!

With sun-kissed skin and salty hair,
We embrace the fun, throw away our care.
Under this sky, we simply sway,
Forever young, come what may.

Captured by the Moonlight

Under the stars, we danced with glee,
A coconut fell right off the tree.
I tripped on my flip-flops, oh what a sight,
You laughed so hard, we lost the night.

The waves whispered secrets, soft and low,
Your towel turned sail, it stole the show.
We made a sandcastle that looked like a troll,
With shells for its eyes, it stole my soul.

While sipping drinks with funny little straws,
You told a joke that earned some applause.
The gulls joined in, squawking with cheer,
In this silly paradise, I felt no fear.

So here we are, on this bright beach chair,
Waving to fish, without a care.
In moonlight's glow, our laughter's spread,
Who knew a shell could match my head?

A Serenade of Island Whispers

The palm trees swayed, an offbeat tune,
As we sang out loud beneath the moon.
A crab joined in, tapping with delight,
Making our concert a comical sight.

The breeze played tricks, ruffled my hair,
While the seagulls swooped down with flair.
I offered them chips, they took the whole bag,
You teased me gently, calling me a brag.

With coconuts clanging like castanets,
We performed our acts, no regrets.
You tripped on your towel, fell on the sand,
And I couldn't help but just laugh, understand?

Each giggle echoed across the sea,
A serenade, just you and me.
In this ridiculous world, love lights our way,
Together we'll dance, come what may!

Radiant Reflections on Still Waters

Casting stones with a plop and a splash,
I aimed for a ripple, but got a big crash.
You giggled aloud, a most charming sound,
As fish swam by, their scales round and round.

The sun settled low, painting skies with gold,
While you told stories, both funny and bold.
I tried to catch frogs that hopped near the shore,
But ended up muddy—who knew there were more?

With ducks as an audience, we played a duet,
You strummed on the banjo, no sign of regret.
But a fish jumped up, took away your hat,
We fell in the water, now how about that?

So let's float on these waves, without any care,
Splashing the ducklings, flying through air.
In reflections of laughter, our joy will grow,
As we skip stones and let the silliness flow!

Love Letters from the Tropics

You wrote me notes in the sand with seashells,
Each letter a giggle, can you hear the bells?
The tide would come in, wash poems away,
But oh, those lost verses, they made my day.

A pigeon delivered a message gone wrong,
A fish slipped out, sang us a song.
We laughed as we tried to send it back home,
Chasing it wildly, through ocean and foam.

Mangoes fell, bursting with juice and delight,
We donned our hats, declaring a fight.
But throwing fruit was a slippery plan,
Now we are covered—what a sticky span!

So here's to our letters from sea to shore,
Each giggle, each trip, we continue to soar.
In this sunny landscape, with mischief and fun,
Your heart's tiny notes are my only one!

A Journey in Lush Green

In a jungle of laughter, I roam,
Bananas in pajamas, far from home.
Mosquitoes dance like they own the night,
While I swat and sway with all my might.

Coconuts tumble, making me jump,
I giggle aloud with each silly thump.
Lizards giggle, they're my best friends,
In this green wonderland, the fun never ends.

Slipping on leaves, what a wild chase,
Flowers are chuckling, still holding their place.
A parrot squawks, "Don't take that route!"
But who needs guidance when I'm out to the max?

With my floppy hat and a cheeky grin,
I join the critters, let the madness begin.
In this verdant playground, life's a big tease,
Every twist and turn makes me giggle with ease.

Surrender to the Sunset Glimmer

As the sun dips low, I spill my drink,
With one last splash, I start to rethink.
The orange sky blinks, "Get your straw in!"
While the waves chuckle, inviting me to swim.

My towel's a canvas, with patterns galore,
It wrinkles and teases, then slides to the shore.
Seagulls giggle as they snatch my fry,
While I wave them off, don't leave me high and dry!

With shades perched on my nose, I strike a pose,
The sunset whispers secrets only he knows.
Dance with the shadows, escape to the light,
I stumble, I giggle, what a silly sight!

So I dive in delight, with sand in my hair,
Who knew a sunset could bring such a flare?
With laughter and splashes, I twirl and I twine,
In the glow of twilight, all worries decline!

Shades of Blissful Escape

In a world painted bright, I take off my shoes,
Dancing with crabs who just can't lose.
With sunglasses on, I strut down the lane,
Those tiny creatures escape with disdain.

Palm trees sway as I strut like a queen,
Banana peels beckon with a grin so mean.
I slip and I slide, laughter fills the air,
Nature's embrace, with no time to spare.

With piña coladas served right on the sand,
I toast to the night, cocktail in hand.
Jumping for coconuts that try to play hard,
But I'm just a kid with the beach as my yard!

So come join my fiesta, with lots of cheer,
Under the stars, we'll dance without fear.
In shades of bliss, where chaos is sweet,
Life's a grand party, down here at my feet.

Unfurling the Heart Like Fronds

With fronds in my hair, I skip through the day,
Those ferns are my friends, come join the fray!
I twirl and I whirl, like a leaf on the breeze,
Each laugh that I share, brings me to my knees.

The sun warms my soul as the waves crash nearby,
A dolphin dives down, gives a wink and a sigh.
It's a wacky adventure in this sunny expansion,
Where whimsy and wonder burst forth in a mansion.

With my sandals flopping and a grin so wide,
I chase after shadows that giggle and hide.
In this carnival garden, joy blooms all around,
A festival of laughter in every sound.

So unfurl your heart, let it float like the mist,
In this comical haven, it's a moment not missed.
With nature as witness, dance like a dream,
In this playful embrace, life's more than it seems!

The Sweetness of Salt and Sand

The waves tickle toes and giggles,
A crab sneaks by with a wiggle.
Coconuts fall with a thud,
While sunbathers roll in the mud.

A seagull swipes my sandwich quick,
Turns out he's more of a sneak than a trick.
The sun's on high, blinding my sleep,
As I dream of treasures buried deep.

I found a shell, but it's empty inside,
Like my wallet after a tourist ride.
The beach is a stage for silly fun,
With loads of laughter, there's always a pun.

With sunscreen slathered on my nose,
I compete with seagulls, who strike a pose.
At sunset, we laugh, dance in the breeze,
'Til it's time to head home, and we say, "Please!"

Beneath the Canopy of Stars

Underneath a twinkling sky,
We roast marshmallows and laugh, oh my!
An octopus called, 'Don't be a fool!'
It's way too late for a night sea school!

A tarp above, our shelter's grace,
Squashed like sardines in this tight space.
A crab walks by, with swagger and pride,
We're giggling so hard, someone almost cried.

The stars look down like a sly old cat,
While we share stories, some silly, some flat.
The waves sing lightly and tease the shore,
While we wonder, is there room for one more?

As the moon blushes, our laughter swells,
We whisper secrets, oh, the things we tell!
With eyes so bright and spirits so free,
We dance with shadows under palm tree.

Forbidden Fruit of the Coast

A mango here, a pineapple there,
I'm an island pirate with no single care.
But biting sweet fruit brings such delight,
As I dodge a pineapple's prickly bite!

Bananas are split with giggles of glee,
As the waves crash, we sip lemon tea.
A fruity fiesta with dances and cheers,
But the blender's broken from too many beers!

The coconut crew swings by with a grin,
Juggling the treasures they brought from the bin.
We cheer them on as they wobble and sway,
Grateful that no one's run away!

With sticky fingers and sand on our face,
We'll dance 'til dawn at this fun little place.
Let's toast to the laughs that never grow old,
In a land where the stories are better than gold!

The Allure of Warm Nights

Moonlight whispers across the bay,
The night's a jester, come out to play.
With fireflies dancing, it's quite the sight,
And we all argue 'bout who squealed in fright!

A hammock sways with a gentle sigh,
While I dream of naps up in the sky.
Someone brings snacks but drops them all,
Now we're all chasing crumbs like a free-for-all!

A breeze jeers softly, pulling me near,
It teases my hair, with a flick and a leer.
The stars above wink in playful jest,
As we sit with our pals, feeling so blessed.

So here's to the nights that come full of cheer,
With laughter and fun that we hold so dear.
When the warm glow fades and the sky turns gray,
We'll carry this joy in our hearts every day!

Captured in the Fragrance of Coconut

In the shade of palm trees, I do sway,
Coconuts roll by, bright as the day.
A monkey steals my hat, what a sight,
I chase him around, oh what a plight!

Sunshine spills on my fruity drink,
A parrot lands, makes me rethink.
"Squawk! You need a hat, it's true!"
I laugh as I sip, with a view so blue.

The beach is alive with silly games,
Sunburns and giggles, who knows our names?
We dance with the waves, carefree and bold,
Finding treasures more precious than gold.

So here in my haven, I take a beat,
Life's a funny dance, feel that warm heat.
When coconuts fall, I just can't resist,
Each moment's a gem, how can I miss?

Melodies of the Coral Reef

Underwater tunes, a fishy choir,
Bubbles rise up like notes of desire.
Octopuses jiggle, and crabs tap dance,
I join in the fun, in a goofy trance!

Sea turtles waddle, slow yet grand,
With shells like disco balls, oh how they stand!
The clownfish laugh, with colors so bright,
I bumble around, what a silly sight!

With every stroke, I bubble anew,
A seaweed wig makes the perfect view.
Sardines swim by, a shimmering haze,
Chasing my fins in a magical daze.

The coral reefs hum, a bizarre beat,
As I dance with the sea, life is oh so sweet.
In this underwater ball, no reason to pout,
It's funny how fish make me want to shout!

Painted Skies and Wandering Souls

The sunset spills colors, a painter's delight,
I try to catch one, with all of my might.
A seagull just giggles, then poops on my cap,
I bow to the sky, this is quite the mishap!

With cotton candy clouds, I roam the scene,
My thoughts drift like kites, so light and keen.
Chasing the breeze, I trip on my feet,
Landing in laughter, life feels so sweet!

The stars peek out, in mischief and glee,
"Did you see that fall?" they whisper to me.
Life's like a canvas, all jumbled and bright,
With strokes of chaos, it feels so right.

So raise up your glasses to the sky so clear,
Paints of joy and the oddest cheer.
For each squiggle and swirl holds a story in tow,
In this funny dance, we let our hearts flow.

Embracing the Whispering Ocean

The ocean whispers secrets, salty and bold,
"Watch out for the wave! It's got stories untold!"
I tumble and roll, like a big sandy ball,
Splashing with laughter, we're having a brawl!

Seashells are treasures, but so full of sand,
I pick one up, slip, and tumble on land.
"Hey, watch where you're going!" the gulls seem to screech,
Laughter erupts like the waves on the beach!

The tide comes a-calling, in rhythm and rhyme,
Dancing with the sea, I lose all notion of time.
With each hearty splash, I embrace this odd fate,
Who knew that the ocean could be so great?

So here's to the merriment found by the shore,
Playing in the waves, who could ask for more?
As moonlight winks down, the fun never ends,
In this watery world, where laughter transcends!

Swaying Silhouettes at Sunset

Palm trees waltz to the breeze's tune,
While crabs strut like they own the dune.
Flip-flops do the cha-cha on sandy feet,
Even the sun melts in this heat.

Cocktails giggle with tiny umbrellas,
Seagulls play tricks on beachside dwellers.
Chasing waves, oh what a ride,
Laughter bubbles like the ocean tide.

The sunset blushes, paints the sky,
While beachballs bounce and seagulls fly.
A tan line quarrel, who's got it worse?
Just sun-kissed souls, no need to curse.

As stars begin their nightly dance,
Even the crickets join in the chance.
Under a blanket of twinkling light,
We sway together, everything feels right.

Mirage of Forgotten Dreams

In the distance, dreams seem to fade,
Like a piña colada that's gone overpaid.
Flip-flops squeak, a curious song,
In this heat, how could you go wrong?

A hammock sways, my trusty steed,
Plans evaporate like a tropical seed.
Forgotten ambitions lie at the shore,
While the tide declares, 'You need nothing more.'

Lizards line dance in the fading rays,
Crabs host parties in their own quirky ways.
As I sip from a coconut's grin,
I ponder if I was ever in it to win.

With each crash of waves, they sing,
About the joys that comfort can bring.
So here I drift, lost in a dream,
Chasing mirages, or so it would seem.

The Dance of Hibiscus and Hope

Hibiscus twirls, a flamboyant flare,
With hopes that flutter in the beachy air.
Breezes tease like a cheeky friend,
Who knew a flower could pretend?

Cockatoos gossip from branches above,
In this paradise, they find love.
While palm fronds swing in a jazzy beat,
Every moment feels fresh and sweet.

Sunsets paint the horizon absurd,
Mirthful colors, it's simply unheard.
The tide whispers secrets to the shore,
As laughter echoes, we ask for more.

Under the moon, the hibiscus giggles,
In this mad whirlwind, my heart wobbles.
With every sway, I chase the glow,
In this dance of dreams, together we flow.

Warmth of the Moonlit Tide

Beneath the moon, where shadows play,
Waves whisper fun in a lulling sway.
Starfish star in the night's parade,
While beach towels become a soft cascade.

Seashells sing tunes of ancient lore,
As socks mingle with sand on the floor.
The lighthouse flickers, a winking eye,
Glimpses of mischief in the sky.

Laughter bounces off the cooling waves,
As jellyfish dance in stylish braves.
In this moonlit realm, under divine,
The tide brings warmth of your hand in mine.

So let's gather secrets, laughter, and fun,
Chase away sorrows until the day's done.
In our little corner, the night feels right,
With the warmth of dreams in the moon's soft light.

Fragments of a Summer's Tale

In flip-flops that squeak, we dash through the sand,
Beneath a sun that can't take a stand.
Ice cream drips down our sun-kissed face,
A sticky debate on the best flavor's grace.

The beach ball wobbles, takes flight with a twist,
A seagull swoops down, oh, how did we miss!
With laughter that echoes from shore to shore,
We juggle our drinks, then drop them galore.

Kites soar above with tails like a rainbow,
While we gracefully fail in our dance with the blow.
Caught in a net of old fishing lines,
We wave to the boaters with goofy designs.

So let's raise a toast, but watch for the spill,
A summer soirée that brings us a thrill.
With every small slip, we cheer and we grin,
In the fragments of laughter, let the fun begin!

Celestial Canopy and Warm Embrace

Beneath the stars, we lay on the ground,
Counting constellations, not making a sound.
A toast to the moon that looks just like cheese,
As crickets compose their symphonies with ease.

Fireflies flash like little shy lights,
Dancing around our flip-flop fights.
With marshmallows toasted, we sing a fine tune,
Our voices a chorus, so silly, so strewn.

A coconut drops from the palm with a plop,
And laughs erupt until someone goes 'shop!'
Wipe the sand from our toes, or so we will try,
But sandy piñatas run under the sky.

In this warm embrace with starlight and mirth,
We capture the essence of unmeasured worth.
With giggles and grins, the night carries on,
In a celestial bliss, till the light of dawn!

Lost Amidst the Banyan Roots

Amidst tangled roots, we wander and roam,
Searching for treasures before we head home.
A curious squirrel, in shades of bright brown,
Mocks us with glee as we stumble down town.

We play hide and seek with the vines as our guide,
But leave it to branches to turn skies wide.
Suddenly trapped, we giggle and squeal,
As the leaves whisper secrets that only we feel.

The echoes of laughter blend with the breeze,
A chorus of mischief that puts us at ease.
With every twist taken, a twist of fate so sweet,
Bouncing around with the roots at our feet.

Through the shade we uncover, oh, what a delight,
Lost in the green, but our hearts feel so light.
With features so silly, like foliage hair,
We dance through the roots without a single care!

Serenade of the Coral Dunes

On coral dunes we prance, a dance like no other,
With shells as our slippers and laughter to smother.
The waves join our rhythm, a splashy refrain,
While we spin and twirl in the warm ocean rain.

A crab with a top hat, oh what a sight!
Winks at our folly, he knows how to bite.
We mimic his moves with a sideways shamble,
A beachside cabaret under the starry scramble.

Biking on sand is no easy feat,
We wobble and tumble, compete with the heat.
An octopus cheers us from his watery dome,
He knows a good party, so let's bring it home!

As dusk paints the sky, we waddle on through,
With memories made that feel fresh and so new.
In this serenade, we'll laugh till we drop,
Our joyful adventure, let's never stop!

Hearts Adrift in Paradise

In a land where coconuts roll,
And sunburns take an unexpected toll,
My heart floats like a wayward boat,
Chasing crabs that dance and gloat.

With flip-flops lost, I do the cha-cha,
A seagull swoops, stealing my nachos,
Laughter erupts with the ocean's roar,
As I spill my drink on the sandy floor.

The palm trees giggle in the breeze,
While I try to impress, but just trip with ease,
A parrot squawks, 'You're quite the sight!'
As I juggle fruit in the fading light.

But in this crazy, sun-kissed ride,
My heart's a fool, but it takes it in stride,
With each wave that crashes in delight,
I wave back to trouble and dance into night.

Gentle Currents of Love

In these waters, hearts do sway,
Like floaties lost in sunbeam play,
A splash of laughter, a tickled toe,
Love is messy, don't you know?

A sunhat flying, caught by a wave,
Chasing romance, like a pirate brave,
But my sunburnt nose gives me away,
As I blush every time you say 'Hey!'

Toes in the sand, we sip on rum,
I tell a joke; it's a total bum,
Yet you giggle and roll your eyes,
As laughter echoes 'neath sunny skies.

In this oasis, where time stands still,
We dance together, a perfect thrill,
With every hiccup, our souls entwine,
In currents swirling, our love will shine.

Nocturnal Echoes of the Shore

Under stars with a coconut grin,
I trip on shells, trying to win,
The dance-off that nobody planned,
With a rogue crab, my unexpected hand.

The moon winks at our silly spree,
As waves sing songs of wild decree,
I shimmied close but lost my grip,
As I attempted an elegant flip.

Laughter rings through the salty air,
With every blunder, we strip despair,
A sea turtle joins in the fun,
Lights on the water, we've just begun.

As the ocean echoes tales of old,
With warmth and friendship, our joy is gold,
In comical stumbles, we find our bliss,
A night to remember, a splash, a kiss.

Eden's Hidden Lullaby

In a garden where bananas grow,
I trip on roots, but love can't slow,
With giggles blooming like summer flowers,
Our silly antics can last for hours.

The mango juice drips down my chin,
While you poke fun, and I just grin,
Caterpillars waltz, teaching me moves,
But I'm all thorns, with no fancy grooves.

When gentle breezes tickle our toes,
I tell a tale only nature knows,
Sloths high above cheerfully yawn,
As we make wishes on every dawn.

In this paradise of laughter and glee,
Where every fumble is meant to be,
We find a rhythm, a sweet, soft sway,
In Eden's laughter, we love and play.

Embrace of the Sultry Sea

In the warm sun, I take a dip,
Where fish parade in a flashy trip.
I wave to crabs with a silly grin,
They scuttle off like they've just seen kin.

The seagulls laugh at my silly splash,
As I trip over waves and make a crash.
They squawk "Look out!" but I can't be seen,
Just another day in my beachy dream.

With sand stuck here and shells in my hair,
I dance like no one, without a care.
Each wave that crashes, brings a new jest,
Oh, how I love this salty fest!

The sun dips low, and I shoo away,
Thoughts of work, here I'll stay.
With a pineapple drink and a goofy grin,
Life in the sun is where I begin.

Lush Temptations

In a garden bright, where the fruits are bold,
I stumble on berries, pure bliss to behold.
I slip on a mango, what a humorless sight,
Just call me 'fruit ninja', I'll win this fight.

Bananas waggle as they laugh and play,
With coconuts chuckling all day.
The papayas giggle, ripe with delight,
In this fruity realm, I feel quite light.

The flowers flirt, petals wave and sway,
I'm the king of this jungle, or so they say.
But bees are buzzing, creating a fuss,
"Stop stealing our nectar!" they start to cuss.

Yet round and round, like a merry-go-round,
These lush temptations keep me spellbound.
With jelly-like laughter, I roll on the ground,
In this jungle of joy, pure bliss is found.

Dance of the Morning Dew

In the dawning light where the dew drops cling,
I twirl like a fairy on a kite's string.
Grass winks at me with its jeweled attire,
As I trip over daisies, fueled by desire.

The sun peeks in with a glowing grin,
"Why so clumsy? Just let it begin!"
I giggle back, with a hop and a skip,
Each droplet bounces, oh, what a trip!

With butterflies swirling in a dizzy dance,
I join their ruckus, caught in a trance.
The chirping birds sing their silly song,
While I'm spinning 'round where I truly belong.

The morning unfolds with laughter so sweet,
Who knew the grass felt good on my feet?
With every soft breeze, I take to the air,
Bumbling and tumbling without a care.

Serene Escapes

In a hammock swinging, I dream of the sky,
The clouds are my friends as they slowly drift by.
But oh, with a lurch, I fall to the ground,
Laughing at life, what magic I've found!

Chasing after butterflies, oh what a sight,
I leap and I bound, feeling so light.
But there's a bee buzzing, it's quite the affair,
"Excuse me!" I yell, in my clumsy despair!

The sunbeams giggle as I slip through the grass,
I'm just a wise fool trying not to pass.
Each rustle and tumble brings joy to my core,
In these serene escapes, who could ask for more?

So here's to the blunders, the slips, and the dives,
In these sunny moments, oh how I thrive!
With a wink to the world, I dance and I sway,
In this blissful paradise, I'll stay and play.

Fading Footprints in Sugar Sand

Upon the shore, we ran with glee,
Chasing crabs as quick as can be.
But every step, oh dear, a slip,
Into the sea, we took a dip!

The sand so warm, it tickles our toes,
Ice cream drips, and that's how it goes.
Seagulls cackle, they steal our fries,
While we laugh under sunny skies.

A beach ball pops, oh what a sound,
We dive to find it lost, then found.
Yet all our treasures just won't last,
As waves come crashing, oh so fast!

So here we stand, with salty hair,
Our laughter ringing in the air.
With fading footprints, tales we weave,
In sugar sand, we laugh and leave.

Shadows of the Island Night

Under the stars, we danced and swayed,
With just a hint of coconut braid.
The fireflies blink, they laugh and tease,
While we try to catch them with ease.

The crickets chirp their silly songs,
As we sing off-key, it can't be wrong.
A lizard leaps, and we all scream,
But then we laugh; it's all a dream.

The moon hangs low, a silly face,
As we trip over each other's grace.
With shadows that twist, run wild and play,
We embrace the night till break of day.

Time flies fast in this island bliss,
Each moment's wrapped in laughter's kiss.
With every stumble, giggles ignite,
In the sweet shadows of the island night.

A Symphony of Mango and Marigold

In a market bright with colors galore,
Mangoes and marigolds, who could ask for more?
We barter and banter, a dance in the heat,
A coconut drop — oops, right at my feet!

The scent of fruit brings big grins wide,
While bees buzz around with much more than pride.
We sip on juices, sticky sweet joy,
With drips on our shirts, what a look to deploy!

We skip through stalls, a rainbow parade,
Trading tall tales of adventures we've made.
A friendly goat steals our snacks from the back,
And we reel with laughter, what a funny quack!

In this savory place where memories unfold,
A symphony crafted in mango and gold.
With marigolds sprouting, we dance in the light,
Creating sweet chaos, oh, what a delight!

Echoes of Laughter in the Waves

Splashing about in the ocean's embrace,
Trying to surf like we own this place.
I wipe out hard and do a funny spin,
The waves just chuckle, inviting me in.

With a floatie tied and sunscreen thick,
We race to the shore like an oceanic trick.
But each big wave brings thrills and falls,
As laughter echoes, bouncing off the walls.

Seashells we gather, treasures so small,
Telling bold stories, oh, we're quite the thrall!
A crab sidesteps, with a wiggle it struts,
"A rival?" I shout, while my friend just guffaws.

With the sun setting low, the sky's aglow,
We splash in the waves, still training to flow.
In this silly carnival, we're all the main stage,
Where laughter lingers and life feels like a page.

Mirages of Deep Blue Dreams

In the land where coconuts sway,
Where flip-flops dance, come what may,
Seagulls giggle, they steal your fries,
As waves throw shade, the sun just sighs.

A llama in a grass skirt spins,
While crabs play cards, betting on fins,
The palm trees gossip, wave hello,
With every breeze, their secrets blow.

The sand's a bed for beach bum dreams,
Where sunscreen's scent blends with ice creams,
And fish in shades of plaid and polka dot,
Are plotting schemes - believe it or not!

So grab your hat and join the fun,
We'll laugh until the day is done,
In this mirage of laughter and glee,
Where reality giggles, and we feel free.

Palette of the Setting Sun

Once a flamingo painted his beak,
With hues that made the parrot squeak,
They strutted down the golden shore,
While turtles laughed, wanting more.

The sun blushed pink, then it took a dive,
As wacky waves started to jive,
The boats, jostling to some rogue beat,
Turned into floating disco suites.

Crabs in sunglasses, looking quite sly,
Were snapping selfies, oh me, oh my!
While dolphins leaped for applause and cheer,
Prepare for laughs, the sunset's here!

In splashes of orange, yellow, and red,
The horizon glowed, like it was fed,
With giggles and whispers from flotsam's glow,
It's a palette of joy, don't you know?

Glimmers of a Blissful Lasting Glow

Beneath the stars, where laughter peaks,
Under moonlight filled with cheeky tweaks,
The hammock swings with a gentle sway,
As parrots party the night away.

A crab in shorts steals the dance floor,
While a starfish wishes he could implore,
For one more spin with a disco ball,
While shells all blush, enjoying it all.

Pineapple hats are all the rage,
As waves dance in a salty stage,
Each twinkle shared and every cheer,
Makes glimmers linger, drawing us near.

So twirl and jump with giddy delight,
This blissful glow, oh what a sight,
With smiles wide and hearts all aglow,
We'll celebrate life, come on, let's go!

In the Arms of Paradise

In a cocoon of chaos and cheer,
Where pineapples laugh with the nearest deer,
We lounge with drinks that dance on our lips,
Making memories with sun-kissed trips.

A flamingo with a floral tie,
Quips about clouds that float too high,
While kites start a bickering spree,
Competing for wind, such a sight to see!

The mermaids trade tales of lost socks,
While hippos bask on their floating blocks,
In this realm where silliness reigns,
We'll dance like no one, free from the chains.

With every splash and every cheer,
In these arms of joy, we're crystal clear,
So let's toast to fun under skies so wide,
For life is a party, come join the ride!

www.ingramcontent.com/pod-product-compliance
Lightning Source LLC
Chambersburg PA
CBHW072221070526
44585CB00015B/1434